$6—
Poe
2/24

Waiting to Unfold

ISBN 978-1-927496-02-2

Cover artwork by Mary Bullington
Edited and designed by Elizabeth Adams

First Edition

Published by Phoenicia Publishing, Montreal
www.phoeniciapublishing.com

Waiting
to
Unfold

Rachel Barenblat

ACKNOWLEDGEMENTS

Some of the poems in *Waiting to Unfold* were previously published, sometimes in earlier form, in the following publications:

"Walking and Falling" and "Night Feeding," *Zeek: A Jewish Journal of Thought and Culture,* June 2010; "Mother Psalm 1," The Jewish Women's Literary Annual, 2011; "Mother Psalm 2," *The Berkshire Eagle,* March 10, 2011; "Belief" and "Carry this in Your Pocket," *Seminary Ridge Review,* fall 2011; "Croup," *CHEST, the official publication of the American College of Chest Physicians,* 2012; "Change," *Hospital Drive,* March 2012; "Fever" and "Comforter," *Bluepepper,* March 2012; "Psalm for the Sixth Day (Mother Psalm 5)," *Spirit Voyages,* April 2012; "Mother Psalm 6," *Calyx,* Vol. 27 no. 2, Summer 2012 and *The Jewish Journal,* January 2013; "Mother Psalm 8," *Bolts of Silk,* September 2012; "Weaning," *Adanna,* issue 2, summer 2012; "Six Weeks," *Em:me,* September 2012; "Besieged," *Earth's Daughters,* 2012; "First Night in Buenos Aires," "New World Order," "Sustenance," and "Push," *Toasted Cheese* 12:3, September 2012; "One Year (Mother Psalm 9)," *The Jewish Women's Literary Annual,* 2012; "Mother Psalm 3," *Wild Violet,* fall 2012; "Grandparents' House," *Shot Glass Journal,* September 2012; "Sleepwear," *Fjords* Vol. 1 issue 4, 2012.

"Little Bean" and "Ready or Not" were set to music by Michael Veloso in 2009 and recorded by Cantilena.

"Eating the Apple" will appear in *The New Promised Land: 120 Contemporary Jewish American Poets,* ed. Matthew Silverman and Debrah Ager (Continuum 2013).

"El Shaddai (Nursing Poem)" will appear in *The Poet's Quest For God,* ed. Oliver V. Brennan and Todd Swift (Eyewear Publishing 2013).

"The Permeable World" will appear in *The Heart of All That Is: Reflections on Home* (Holy Cow! Press, 2013).

Many of these poems originally appeared, sometimes in earlier forms or with different titles, at the blog Velveteen Rabbi.

For Drew
whose arrival transformed me

Contents

Introduction

The first year of new parenthood is unfamiliar territory, and since no two experiences are the same, there's no map. When one's sleep schedule and sense of self are thrown off-kilter, as inevitably happens, it's natural to cling to something familiar. I clung to poetry.

When the baby was born, there was no space for anything else. Jason Shinder, of blessed memory, used to say "Whatever gets in way of the work, is the work." If motherhood were going to get in the way of poetry, then it would become the substance of poetry.

During the first year of our son's life, I wrote one poem each week. In those early months, that one poem was the only writing I managed to do. I shared the poems with friends and with blog-readers, which kept me (however tenuously) tethered to my own creative life.

Parenting an infant is emotional, exhausting, hilarious. So the poems are too. Here are overwhelm and amazement, gratitude and frustration. The diagnosis of postpartum depression, the road to recovery, our son's first gestures and his first steps.

When I was a student chaplain, my colleagues told me that parenting was a theological education which would make me a better rabbi. Being a mom does make me a better rabbi. I don't know whether it makes me a better poet than I would otherwise be, but I hope it might.

Through revisions, these poems remain my chronicle of a journey I would otherwise have forgotten. Banal and miraculous, the most universal and the most particular. Both the parenthood and the poetry are journeys I'm glad to be on. Thanks for coming along for the ride.

Letters to Little Bean

LITTLE BEAN (ONE)

I don't like to cough too hard,
to move too fast.
Something twinges
and I'm afraid I'll shake you loose,
little bean.

How can I convince you
not to jump ship?
Some mother I am, already
conflating you with the sibling
that wasn't.

Every morning
I talk myself through
pushing the thin needle
into my skin.
If it keeps you here…

I don't believe
in making bargains
with God, but
I'm making one now
with every breath.

If my mother
could hear this
she would laugh and cry
like a fragile bird shaking
it never gets easier.

LIGHT (TWO)

You've graduated
from aspirin to raisin
grape to olive
to the size of a lime
or small dense plum

you have fingers
and toes, though
no longer a tail
you're not an embryo
anymore

the books tell me
you are translucent
there are pictures
I imagine light
shining through you

in Hebrew, "skin" and "light"
are homonyms
the sages say we'll wear light
like a garment
in the world to come

the *midrash* says
in my womb
you know all the Torah
anyone could ever know
deep in your unformed bones

but when you breathe
your first taste of this world
you'll forget
as I've forgotten
we can learn together

INTRODUCTION (THREE)

Asked to introduce myself
in seven words
I come up with
"growing a new poem
line by line."

Six months
until we meet.
Your father and I
putter with paint chips,
marvel at tiny clothes.

You turn backflips
in your own salt sea.
Stay safe in there.
Learn what you can.
We're waiting.

APPROACHING (FOUR)

First thing this morning
I feel you flutter
and smile at the ceiling, relieved:
still in there, still moving—
good sign, kid. Keep it up.

Someday I'll dash to the crib
to make sure you're breathing.
By then the goldenrod
will be shorn, the ground
tucked in to its white sleep.

What will it be like, I wonder
to grow up with a mother
who cranks Finnish pop music
to polish the silver
before Rosh Hashanah?

Will you help me?
Or maybe you'll roll your eyes
when I say it's like *teshuvah*,
cleaning away the tarnish
so what's beneath can gleam.

I rein in my imagination:
thirteen weeks yet
before we can even touch you
much less plunge headlong
toward first grade.

I talk to you out loud
while driving my car,
hand wedged between my seatbelt
and the wall of my belly.
I say: it's a good world out here.

IMPERMANENCE (FIVE)

Today I'll finish our sukkah
stacking old wildflowers
to hint at roof, twining tinsel
around the slats

all year we imagine
our houses are our houses
stable and comfortable
waterproof and familiar

but these seven days
remind us that permanence
is overrated, that our true home
is under the stars

change is always underway
nine short weeks remain
until you'll leave the home
you probably think is forever

and enter our world
airy and unpredictable
where we won't know what you need
even when you tell us

your first big leap of faith, kid:
into nothing you've ever known
into the fragile sukkah
we've decorated just for you

READY OR NOT (SIX)

Less than a month now
until we meet face to face
skin to skin

when you squirm in my hands
will I recognize the movements
I felt from the inside

your tiny dolphin body
surfacing and then curling
back beneath my sea?

your little world
is as ready as I can make it
your crib wears new sheets

the borrowed breast pump
waits to be useful
I hope I am useful

let me cup my hands
around your flickering flame
in December's deepening dark

ALMOST (SEVEN)

To think you're coming
in two short days
is as implausible
as a plan to sprout wings
and sail off our hill

I've grown accustomed
to holding you inside me
feeling your every move
as though my own heart
knocked against my ribs

I can hardly imagine
what will be required
to bring you forth
much less what comes
after

holding you
nourishing you
learning to swaddle
and change diapers
and read your moods

today the cat perches
on my desk, near my hands
gazing at me gravely
she knows
some big change is coming

NEWBORN (EIGHT)

After nine long months
you're my little bean again:
my belly was ponderous
but you are tiny

on the blank page of your crib
you're a punctuation mark
you fit in your daddy's arm
like a precious football

already your brow furrows
with worry lines
we ache to soothe, as though
we could keep you in Eden

sleep debt piles up like laundry
but who could fail to marvel?

Waiting to Unfold

EL SHADDAI (NURSING POEM)

Was God overwhelmed
when Her milk first came in

roused by our thin cries
for compassion?

She'd birthed creation
from amoebas to galaxies

but did She expect to see
Her own changeability

mirrored behind our eyes?
Nothing could have prepared Her

for the shift from singularity
to multiplicity.

And the blank-faced angels
offered their constant praise

without understanding Her joy
or the depth of Her fear.

NEWBORN SESTINA

I'm mesmerized by his form
even when he rouses me in the dark.
Nurse, burp, time for a change
then nurse again: it's all new,
this rhythm, his needs.
And for now, I'm his all:

source of milk, familiar sounds, all
the comforts of home. He forms
cries reedy and grizzled, need
which clenches my heart dark
and fearful. I never knew
my sense of God would change

but I see now that You are change
and these moments are holy, all
the ways he's always new.
Hard to believe his compact form
spent nine months in the dark
of my womb, every need

met. I'm not sure what I need:
sleep, soothing, maybe a change
in perspective these dark
December days. For a time all
is well, but then I try to form
a sentence, an idea, something new

and my words trail off. The new
year will bring endless need
but I want to think we can form
a way through, a path to change
for everyone in this house, all
of us making our way in the dark.

Creator of light and dark,
every day You continually renew
the work of creation, all
the tiny miracles we need,
surprises and change.
Help my hands and heart to form

what these dark days need,
to embrace the new, meet change
with all the grace of this tiny form.

NIGHT FEEDING

Three in the morning:
you're curled on my shoulder

like a hermit crab out of its shell,
warm as a blanket out of the dryer

when I lift you down from your perch
your dark eyes are wide open

as a hind longs for water
my soul longs for sleep

but I pace the round carpet
until I can crawl into bed

praying that I get a whole hour
before you summon me with your cries

which call in equal measure
my milk and my tears

SIX WEEKS

the changes leave me
gobsmacked

baby shouldered
and wibbling,

froth at the corner
of his cupid's-bow mouth

stretch marks
like a tiger-print tattoo

marking my belly
fertile

days distilled simple:
nurse, diaper, repeat

some day soon
you'll smile

and these sundered nights
will be redeemed

BESIEGED

Seven weeks in
I am rubble, strafed
by a round-cheeked pilot
who attacks at random
with his air-siren wail

I lie in bed
pleading with no one
for just one hour
but the monitor crackles
and deals its death blow

yet once he's milk-faced
and sleepy, head lolling
in the crook of my arm
I fall in love with the enemy
all over again

his imperious voice
and grabby hands, his eyes
like slate marbles
and his endless hunger
never satisfied

POWER

But most of all
       new parenthood requires
              an endless stream of batteries

for the vibrating chair
       with its bright medley
              of earworm nursery rhymes

for the mobile, Mozart
       sparking synapses
              while the baby sleeps

for the baby monitors
       like walkie-talkies
              which brook no reply

but when the gadgets
       run down or fail
              all we have are hands

voices, shoulders, breasts
       running on reserve power
              we didn't know we had

LEGLESS

The sadness arises
again
and cuts my legs
out from under me

the monotony
of trying to soothe
screams as frequent
as the waves...

I'm tethered,
my body is harnessed
my own desires
pushed aside

sometimes he stares
up at my eyes
as though
he sees me

but then
his chin crumples
resolute and furious
and I disappear

2AM FEEDING

Moonlight slants across the floor
as I scuff down the stairs to your yellow room

you've thrashed loose from your swaddling
and scooted halfway down the mattress

fists clenched and mouth open
in a caricature of fury

the moment you attach your face goes slack
and unconcerned, eyes shut, one brow raised:

tiny Vulcan, commenting with a silent gesture
on humanity's quirks and misconceptions

what will you recall of these long nights
when I watched the moon cast shadows on snow?

WALKING AND FALLING AT THE SAME TIME

Remember the warm flat river
which smelled like walnuts,

the hum of the motor idling
the peel of wet rope through your hands

how it felt to bob, cradled
in the life jacket's embrace

then the boat would pick up speed
and you'd rise out of the water

feeling it thrum underfoot
as the cliffs whirled by

falling asleep is that way too
you have to learn how to float

in these warm waters, to hold fast
to the rope towing you forward

until the great green world blurs
and you fly away

MOTHER PSALM 1

A psalm of anticipation

Even now, the hills frosted
like children's corn flakes,
summer's wild effusion waits
in the wings. As we walk
on eggshells past the nursery
the promise of a night's sleep
gleams just beyond our grasp.
Hidden in your babbling patter
are the words you can't yet speak.
All the seeds are curled tight
but I believe with a perfect faith
that they will open; I know
beneath the snow red tulips
are forming. Today plate glass
presses me like a dead flower
but soon I'll pop in three dimensions.
I crown you with baby oil
and fold tomorrow after tomorrow
into your clenched fists.

BELIEF

The days will lengthen
the voice of the veery thrush
will be heard on our land

the tiny stars of crocuses
well-rested from the long dark
will adorn the icy mud of spring

the sap already rising
will feed a million tiny banners
unfurling across the hills

and this small blue pill
will banish anxiety, restore to me
the woman I only dimly remember

laughing in photographs
with her hand on her round belly
hope curled inside, waiting to unfold

CHANGE

At four in the morning
my body is sleep-heavy
but my heart
isn't an imploded star.

Breakfast tastes good
again, oatmeal
for my milk supply, Clementine
like a handheld sun.

I choose music
over silence, the baby's
Shar-pei soft head
beneath my palm.

My eyes still sting
sometimes, the wide world
reduced to the nursery,
the living room couch.

My pill bottle rattles.
Blessed are you
who revives the deadened,
I say, and swallow hard.

MOTHER PSALM 2

A psalm of anticipation

I forgot to hang the feeder.
The cat never settled on the couch
to watch the chickadees and juncos
at their perennial cocktail party.
Next year you'll be old enough
to notice as they congregate.
For now, settle into your stroller
and listen: as the equinox approaches
the woodpeckers are waking.
You can't see the trees' distant fingers,
too far and fine for your new eyes,
but a trillion twigs are turning nubbly
like grapestems denuded of fruit
and inside lurk embryonic leaves.
On your eighth day, flakes fell
thick and fast, coating hills
which haven't yet been bared, but
soon the snow will seep into soil
revealing the pale and sun-starved lawn.
Your short life has held only winter.
As you can smell milk when I hold you
I can smell the earth warming, the mud
laced with shreds of last year's mulch,
the spring I know is almost here.

SLEEPWEAR

I want to burn that bra
my husband says, plucking

at my nursing-compliant
weird fetish brassiere

this new-mother costume
matronly as a girdle

all night I fumble to reveal
what the baby gropes for

my breasts have become
utilitarian as beer kegs

and if we dare to touch
the infant alarm goes off

someday he'll move on
to cereal and applesauce

and I'll cup my curves
in turquoise and magenta

will I recognize
the woman in the mirror

stretch marks faded silver
beneath unfamiliar silk?

FIRST NIGHT IN BUENOS AIRES

Old political cartoons punctuate the pink walls.
Our waiter wears black tie, brings out dish after dish:

steaks the size of dinner plates, homemade noodles
and lettuce with vinegar, sweet onion on the side.

We cap the day with bright limoncello
and a wobbly walk on cobblestones, like Europe, refracted.

By breakfast — coffee, *medialunas* smeared with *dulce*,
watching the city wake through wrought-iron doors —

two cells have collided inside me, beginning
their long journey into the wide world

and we set off on foot to explore,
never dreaming what adventures lie ahead.

NEW WORLD ORDER

I slam on the brakes
        and the crockery in the back seat
                slides forward with a crash

unpacking the dishes
        in my sister's kitchen I weep
                as though they mattered

the next day
        a mental thread snags
                on the calendar's sharp edge

and I realize my body
        is already at work
                forming you

I choose grape juice
        for my four cups of joy
                not yet able to imagine

your squeals of delight
        as I chant the fifteen steps
                from kindling the candles

to singing Had Gadya,
        the unfamiliar joys
                of our newly-disordered lives

CARRY THIS IN YOUR POCKET

For the sake
of your sternum
rising and falling,
the deep folds
in your thighs,
your peach fuzz
beneath my palm
the whole world
was created

every domino
tipping the next:
my young father
playing the bugle
and flirting with
his movie star
at summer camp,
paper cigar ring
on her finger—

every thing leads
to you standing
in the exersaucer
on your tiptoes
damp fists clenched
humming to yourself
in a language
which only God
can understand

MOTHER PSALM 3
A psalm of anticipation

Raise your legs, then let them fall
again and again as though you knew
turning over is just a twist
and roll away. Do you remember
somersaults in the warm recesses
of the womb, suspended weightless
like an astronaut on his tether?
Sometimes you kick for long minutes
without stopping, now as then, though
the sensation is lost to me except
in the dreams I visit between feedings.
A few warm days and suddenly
the icebound troughs of winter
are as implausible as pregnancy.
The birches go first, and the willows
a haze of green and gold
on the verge of bursting free,
a new world already almost here.

BEAUTY PARLOR

The first haircut is a revelation.
After months of scraggly and milk-stained
suddenly I'm light as the air
whispering across my nape.

I remember turning foam curlers
into a dragon while my mother tipped her head
into the shampoo sink, regal and relaxed.
Now she jiggles my son in her lap

singing "bye bye, blackbird"
as I allow myself to be transformed.
His first time beneath the Texas sky:
What beauty will he remember?

SUSTENANCE

The taqueria doubles as a car wash.
You're asleep in the backseat
when we pull in. Sun glints
off of tinted Suburban windows.

Iced tea in a Styrofoam cup
too big for our rented cup-holders.
The flour tortillas are homemade
and the salsa tingles my tongue.

Next year we'll sit at a Formica table
and cut a bean-and-cheese into wedges
your pudgy fingers can hold.
We'll wipe your ecstatic face clean.

Now all we can do is rave quietly
about this dingy corner of heaven
and drive away, keeping secret
what sustenance remains in store.

TASTE

This thin gruel is your first step
toward strawberries warm from the sun

wedges of cheddar made from grassy milk
Macs and Cortlands pressed into cider

but once this spoon passes your lips
I have to curb mine from proclaiming

I made every ounce of exuberant you,
your chubby thighs and chipmunk cheeks

hesitation stills my hand, but
you don't know what bittersweet means

what blessing should I make
over this first bite, your open mouth

a door to the wide world waiting
to be brought inside?

EATING THE APPLE

The first time
I spoon applesauce

your long shiver
makes me laugh

one bite, then
you turn away

this new flavor
not yet familiar

in my imagination
I'm introducing you

to mangoes already,
to fresh bread,

halvah and tamales,
injera and kimchi

but you're not
ready for difference

or new discovery,
hot fists clinging

to the Eden
you've always known

CROUP

The angel who taught you Torah
in the comfort of the womb
might have warned you

the world holds this too:
night stretching endless,
your breathing labored

every hoarse and broken cry
a wordless plea for comfort
no one here can give, but

the tap above your lip
just before you emerged
into this great wide open

made that otherworldly wisdom
recede, and all I can offer
as you bury your face in my neck

is the ache in my chest
to match yours, my murmured
request for healing

ascending like water vapor
and dissipating
into the listening skies

CRESTING THE FIRST HILL

The rollercoaster   picks up speed
you assume boat pose   straining to sit

you discover   new vowels, try
the kick and roll   open your mouth wide

Half a year ago   you emerged slick
one skinny fist   clenched and bluish

now when I bend   to kiss your belly
your eyes crinkle   and you grab my hair

my glasses, whatever's   within reach
we zoom downhill   toward who you'll become

FIRST DAY

We'll cross the asphalt holding hands:
a flying leap
toward a moving trapeze

or maybe your backpack
will rest at my feet
until the bus arrives

then the empty house

will my chest echo like a drum
as I bend to pick up toys,
the flotsam of our life together?

through the long quiet
I'll startle at every cry
from the cat, from the birds

waiting for someone
to need me

REPETITION

refuse to let go
grip my finger tight
bang your feet on the floor
blow raspberries at the sky

grip my finger tight
pop off the breast and beam
blow raspberries at the sky
toe off a small red sock

pop off the breast and beam
lie on your back and babble
toe off a small red sock
crinkle a book made of cloth

lie on your back and babble
open mouth, insert world
crinkle a book made of cloth
rub your reddening eyes

open mouth, insert world
insist you are not sleepy
rub your reddening eyes
cling to your giraffe

insist you are not sleepy
grip my finger tight
cling to your giraffe
refuse to let go

MOTHER PSALM 4
A psalm of expansion

Trying to sit up is hungry work.
I praise your abs for doing their part,
I settle you on the pillow in my lap
and as you draw shefa down from its source
your eyes flutter shut, your breathing slows.
Nothing else I know can match this comfort:
the steady flow of warm milk, my hand
stroking the curve of your head, your belly
pressed to my ribcage, the gentle rhythm
as each of us inhales and then lets go.
Daily I expand how much I can love
your toes, your cough, your raised eyebrow.
It feels dangerous, prying my chest open
to make room for everything that's new
and you're in the world now, the risks
as numerous as the stars in the sky,
but with fear come delights, too—
your face smeared with prunes
almost too luminous for me to bear.
Each day your glee polishes my dull edges
and I shine. As I grew your body
you changed mine. My heart stretches.
I think I might resent these silvery scars
if you weren't grabbing for my hair,
my glasses, reminding me how much there is
to reach for, to marvel at, everywhere.

IN THE WATER

gulls and pelicans wheeled and cried
below the balcony

morning and evening the cloth umbrellas
unfurled and furled like hibiscus

and daily I walked onto the beach
in my maternity tankini

and entered the water gratefully
imagining you afloat in my small sea

oh, baby, when you are grown
will we reminisce about the old days

when a pregnant woman could still swim
off the soft rippled edge of Texas?

MOTHER PSALM 5
A psalm for Friday

On the sixth day I labored
to birth a world.

To make room for you
I contracted myself, touched

the place where I disappear.
And for you, the journey

from my endless embrace
into the world of separation...

But when my work was completed
I gazed into your bottomless eyes

—my image; my likeness—
and I was not alone

rest with me now
and remember.

MOTHER PSALM 6

A psalm of revelation

Don't chew on your mama's tefillin
I say, dislodging the leather
from your damp and eager grasp.
We play peekaboo beneath my tallit,
hiding your face and revealing it
the way God is sometimes present
sometimes not. You like the drums,
the fiddle and clarinet.
You bang your rattle on the floor.
As we sing "Praise God,
all you elders and young children"
you bellow and and we laugh.
During silent prayer your yearning
opens my floodgates.
When the Torah is carried around
I waltz you in my arms, my own scroll.
All my prayers are written
in your open face.

MESSAGES

in the curve of your head,
its whorls of soft hair

in your grasping hands
and your dolphin trills

some of your signals
are plain as speech—

your staccato kicking,
a fist pressed to your eyes

—but no one can decipher
your most secret heart

COMFORTER

you wake in your crib's embrace
from the dream of a distant heartbeat

a voice says cry out!
and you cry out

bewailing the tragedy of separation
until I gather you to my breast

glowing numbers shift silently
and your desperation eases

someday you'll learn to fumble soft stars
into their places

to nuzzle your giraffe
and count adinkra like talismans

but for now I am consolation
I make the rough places plain

THESE ARE A FEW

Sitting up
beats lying down

like a lotion rubdown
beats a dose of vitamins

like peach yogurt
beats spinach puree.

Mylar balloons
filled with helium:

even better than
a stream of water

that splashes past
your grabby hands.

My palm stroking your head,
your arms around my neck.

In the morning,
the baby in the mirror

kicking his feet
to see you again.

THRONE OF GLORY

O changing table! Your terrycloth breast rises and dips like the
gentle swell of the hills. Underneath, Pampers, stacked like stones
in a falling-down wall beside a box filled with damp tufts of cloud.
Above, the bright elephant hovering in the sky, its mirrored belly
reflecting emptiness. Someday you will retire to the basement and
mice will dart beneath your sheet. Will you remember feet beat-
ing a tattoo on your chest, hands questing for the safety belt which
dangles into your ribcage? Will you recall the scent of pink Johnson
& Johnson's, this woman's hands, this baby's gleeful laughter? What
will you dream?

PHANTOM BABY

The biggest change:
        even when we're apart
                I'm not self-contained

always aware
        that you washed up
                helpless on my shore

strangers squint
        as I narrate my day
                in a sing-song to no one

the sticky smudges
        you left on my glasses
                frame everything I see

high-pitched voices
        make me turn, heart
                suddenly inside-out

you are missing
        from my hip
                an invisible ache

LOOKING AHEAD

Someday you'll know us by our cars:
you'll report that mama's
is blue, that dad's is a black truck.

Maybe you'll want to look inside,
to decode the tanks and hoses,
this one the size of a pineapple

and that one filled with antifreeze,
relishing the dark smudge of oil
that moistens your hands. Or maybe

you'll gravitate toward the yard:
petting pussywillows' spring silk,
blowing dandelions to smithereens,

checking the pots on the deck
as you wait for herb seeds to sprout.
Whatever speeds your heart

don't be afraid to go deep:
step on stones in summer streams
in search of swimming holes

or dive into sci-fi paperbacks'
lurid covers and dry newsprint pages,
calling distant galaxies home.

When you come up for air, marvel
at where you've been, where
you still have yet to go.

HAND-ME-DOWNS

My knife zips through tape
and the box unfolds its wings.
I lift little pockets of emptiness,
their sleeves carefully tucked.

Each of these an embrace
in jersey knit, in waffle weave
or flannel, snug turtlenecks
and button-downs. This red one—

short-sleeved, blazoned
with the alphabet—urges me
to measure each day: fall is coming,
bright goldenrod and schoolbuses

and soon sleeveless rompers
will seem as implausible
as the idea that you were ever
small enough to wear

what I place now
in a box which once held Pampers.
The packing tape screeches.
I seal the summer away.

FEVER

You're on fire beneath my lips,
hot as the coal that Moshe grabbed
when the angel forced his hand.
As we rock in the dark
I want to pray for healing
but I'm muddled with sleep.
I sing to you in two holy tongues.
You whimper. My eyes are closed
but I have known your face
since it first appeared, blurred
and grainy, on the ultrasound screen.
When I replace you on cool sheets
you cry out once and then curl
clutching yellow bunny in one hot hand.
The white noise machine croons.
What do your fever dreams show you?
How long will you remain a furnace,
incandescent in my arms
and exhausted from the burning?

A SWEET YEAR

No honey until you're a year old, but
I can pop the seal on a pint
of last year's applesauce.

The afternoon light was thick and gold
the day we cored a bushel and a peck,
hands sticky and kitchen fragrant.

The jars were earmarked: for latkes,
for breakfast, and for you—
whoever you might turn out to be.

I remember resting my palm on my belly.
I can't remember not knowing
your voice, your eyes, my expanded heart.

MOTHER PSALM 7

A psalm of repetition

Three times a day I lift the tray table
from its moorings, unsnap your plastic bib
and carry them both to the same kitchen sink
where I bathe you. A few swipes of soapy sponge
and both come clean, half-eaten blueberries
and fallen cheerios (dinner's debris, evidence
of the excited swipe of your fist) swirling
into the drain's aluminum basket. This week
you prefer rotini to purees. You answer us
with chanted vowels, embellishing with trills.
You tip your head to one side, beaming, then
wave to your breakfast, to your mother,
to the colored bowls you like to knock together
to hear their percussive sounds. Some days
grind like a broken mobile from the start:
barely out of the crib and you're already cranky,
refusing sleep's comfort because you can't bear
the world going on without you. But we make it
to the finish line (pear yogurt, open mouth)
and then the slate's washed, you're in PJs
and I remember again that everything's temporary.
Your tired tears may endure for the night
but breakfast comes in the morning. Child,
I dress you in gladness; sing praises, open wide.

WEANING

You push me away
and reach for the bottle.

Once in Scotland I parted
spongy turf with my fingers

and water welled up like sorrow
its source unknown.

In my childhood playhouse
the table was always set

for guests who never came.
Already my body is shrinking.

You settle like a little king
into the crook of my arm

one hand seizing
the plush belt of my bathrobe

the other splayed
across the warm cylinder.

Your lashes drift down
and your restless legs still

exactly as they did
when I was everything.

THE PERMEABLE WORLD

All the world is a room made of windows
with different views through every pane

sit with me, knock two bowls together
hold an etrog carefully in both hands

watch me gather palm and myrtle and willow
and turn in every direction, hoping for gifts

from the winds that quake the aspen,
from the earth, from the spiraling fire

last Sukkot you were snug inside, but
now you've joined the permeable world

when the rains come the roof leaks
but you're safe in my arms

and at night we're surrounded by angels
twinkling on all sides, escorting us through

CHOICE

In the beginning we had to choose
to open my body to possibility

to move furniture, paint walls
fold implausibly small kimono shirts

try to shelve our uncertainty
and number our anticipated losses...

I can barely remember. The solid fact
of you clapping your hands

has overwritten those old files
leaving no trace of what was beneath.

This week your syllable is ma-ma-ma
the new name I inherited

when I wrestled with labor
and you, little blessing, slipped free.

MOTHER PSALM 8

A psalm of transition

When all else fails, a stroll will put you to sleep.
We walk beneath trees still mostly green, here
and there a branch burst into purple flame, until
Whole Foods looms glossy at the sidewalk's end.
We load into the basket beneath your sleeping form
a pumpkin and a gourd hooked like a swan's neck.
All the way there my sister and I talk about marriage
and I wonder with whom you'll walk like this someday
remembering aloud the house you grew up in, our
spiral staircases, the boxes of dolls in the basement.
The minute we stop, you wake; I pepper your head
with kisses, try to adjust your already-drooping socks.
It's autumn in Newton. My muddy iced coffee is the last
of the season. Little man, you can move yourself now
across the floor with intent, though you pause and sit
contemplating whether the ball that's rolled away
is worth the effort of the journey. It's always worth
the effort of the journey: the ball, the book, the child
you may someday try to raise, as clueless as we.
Make your way across the room. Pluck sweetness
from every interaction, extract smiles from strangers.
Go get it: we're cheering each painstaking step you take.

FEARS

I can't wrap you in gauze.
The world is sharp.

Someone will hurt you
and I won't be there to swoop you up.

Your tender heart will be broken
in ways no one can repair.

Or we'll hurt each other.
You'll yell that I don't understand.

The words "I hate you"
will be your rusty knife.

Long after you leave the room
I'll be dazed from what I've lost.

CHILDPROOFING

Wooden slats. U-bolts. Swinging hinges.
Sheets of transparent plastic. Plastic plugs
pushing their way inside every socket.
Fiddly gadgets to catch doors and drawers
before they reveal their vulnerable insides. And you

trundling across the floor, chasing
the ball that plays the same three measures
of classical music again and again,
sleuthing out hidden electrical cords. We can't
pad every surface: you whack your head

on the undersides of bookshelves, on
the coffee table, on the legs of a chair
you didn't realize you'd crawled beneath.
Sometimes if you catch us watching you wail.
Sometimes you barrel on, intent

on whatever's rolled just beyond your grasp.
When you fall we offer the comfort
of familiar arms—or distraction: look, the cat!
Too soon you push away. The world calls.
You turn the corner and recede from view.

CHASING THE BALL

The kettle on the stove whistles a low, slow tune
as you circuit from nursery to hallway to kitchen
and back again, chasing a rattling ball.

When you catch up to it, you throw it forward again
and I remember all of the goals I tossed ahead
and aimed for (grimly or with joy)—

as soon as your body learned to be warm
we'd be able to dress you for nightfall
in fewer than four layers of wool and fleece

someday you'd focus on my face, someday
the binary of sleeping or screaming would fan out
into a spectrum of possibilities...

I didn't know to anticipate your glee
when I pick you up, count to three, then
turn you so the world is upside-down

or your determined grip on the xylophone mallets
too big for you to wield, how you change course
and kneel up to bang on the wooden keys instead

now when you say ma-ma-ma I tell you that's my name
and look, there's daddy, that's the cat, do you want
your ball? Soon your babble will coalesce

and then what? I can't even imagine what's coming.
The rising sun casts the hills in pink. I sip my tea.
You barrel ahead. All I can do is follow.

PUSH

The nurses taught us to pin and tuck
a thin blanket into a straitjacket

each night when bedtime arrived
your dad would kneel over you on the rug

now you sleep limp like an old rag doll
your twiga and your plush rabbit akimbo

but when you're awake you push back
against baby gates and mountainous stairs

if I've chosen the wrong foods
or if I'm not paying enough attention

you scatter what's on the tray
then glance at me sly and sideways

no, I don't want to clean shells
and cheese off the kitchen floor, but

secretly I love to watch you
stretch your wings

you're a chimera, half dad and half mom
and all you, from your furrowed brow

to your feet fighting to break forth
from the terrible tyranny of socks

claim your birthright and your blessing
unlock every strap and burst free

AND THEN THERE ARE THE DAYS

when nothing is easy
your dad drives away at dawn
you wail through your diaper change
the formula in your bottle is too hot
you push my hands away and flail your feet
when I try to fasten your corduroys

the days when you decide that naps
are for other babies
and the cat's tail looks enticing
and none of the food I put on your tray
appeals to you at all, except the cheese
and maybe the sliced banana

and the stroller is confining
but the floors of our house are dull
you've already crawled every inch
of this kitchen, it holds no secrets
and the Hungarian dvds won't play
and darkness falls too soon

when you howl through the potluck
and throw your Cheerios on the floor
and I try to tell the other parents
he's not usually like this
but they don't believe me
though at least they are kind

even on days when I can't wait
to glide your pocket door shut
and pour myself a fishbowl of red wine
my heart still swells two sizes
as I collect the colored plastic cups
you've strewn across the living room

GRANDPARENTS' HOUSE

Your hands slap the marble floor.
Your voice fills the empty spaces
in this house I never grew up in.

You tug your sun hat off your head
and squint at the vast Texas sky.
Your hands slap the marble floor.

Clutching bits of flour tortilla
you beam, face smeary and bright.
Your voice fills the empty spaces.

Bang on the windows, little boy:
your reflection is everywhere you look
in this house I never grew up in.

THANKSGIVING

Last year I carried you inside
to the buffet, to the table
to the big blue birth ball
where I bounced beside the fire.

Now you scramble speedy
around the living room, wind up
in Downward Dog by accident,
grab and devour bits of turkey.

Your babble, your crinkled eyes,
your hot hand slapping mine,
your gasps of laughter
even the year of staccato nights

and the painful realignments
of a marriage shifting
to new foundations:
all I can do is give thanks.

ONE YEAR (MOTHER PSALM 9)

A psalm of ascent

When the doctor brought you
through my narrow places
I was as in a dream: tucked behind
my closed eyes, chanting silently
we are opening up in sweet surrender.
The night before we left the hospital
I wept: didn't they know
I had no idea what to do with you?
Even newborn-sized clothes
loomed around you, vast and ill-fitting.
I couldn't convince you to latch
without a nurse there to reposition.
But we got into the car, the old world
made terrifying and new, and
in time I learned your language.
I had my own narrow places ahead,
the valley of the postpartum shadow.
Nights when I would hand you over,
mutely grateful to anyone willing
to rock you down, to suffer your cries…
But those who sow in tears
will reap in joy, and you
are the joy I never knew I didn't have.
I have paced these long hours
and now I am home in rejoicing,
bearing you, my own harvest.

adinkra - symbols used by the Akan of Ghana, each of which represents a proverb or aphorism

dulce - Spanish for "sweet," this is an abbreviation for dulce de leche, a kind of caramel made from milk sugar

El Shaddai - a Hebrew name for God which comes from the root meaning "breasts"

etrog - also known as a citron, this nubbly and fragrant fruit is used for ritual purposes during the festival of Sukkot

Had Gadya - this Aramaic song (the title means "One little goat" or "One little kid") is sung at the end of the seder (the Passover meal)

halvah - a sweet candy frequently made from sesame seeds (the name is the same in both Hebrew and Arabic)

injera - a yeasted Ethiopian flatbread with a uniquely spongy texture and fermented flavor

kimchi - traditional Korean dish made of fermented vegetables

medialunas - the Spanish word for crescent-moon-shaped rolls or croissants

midrash - exegetical stories which explain and interpret Torah

salsa - the Spanish word for "sauce," this term colloquially refers to a spicy condiment

shefa - a Hebrew word meaning abundance of blessing, that which pours down from God into creation

sukkah - a small hut or booth, a temporary structure built for use during the festival of Sukkot, when Jews dine (and sometimes sleep) in these impermanent dwellings for one week (plural: sukkot)

Sukkot - the festival during which Jews enjoy being in their sukkah; a harvest festival; a remembrance of the Exodus from Egypt.

tallit - the Hebrew word (the Yiddish word is tallis) for prayer shawl

tamales - a traditional Mesoamerican dish made of masa, a corn-based dough, wrapped in leaves and steamed, often filled with protein (stewed meat, beans, etc)

taqueria - a restaurant where tacos are sold

tefillin - also known as phylacteries, these are small leather boxes on long leather straps. The boxes contain passages from scripture, and are worn (one bound to the forehead, one to the arm) during weekday prayer.

teshuvah - the Hebrew word for repentance or return

tortillas - Mexican flatbreads, cooked on a griddle

twiga - the Swahili word for giraffe

Afterword

I could not have written this manuscript without the help of many friends, readers, and loved ones. Thanks are due first and foremost to Ethan Zuckerman, my husband, for joining me in this adventure. (And, of course, to our son Drew.) I am also grateful to my spiritual director Rabbi Nadya Gross, who suggested that I try writing mother psalms; to my mother-in-law who went above and beyond the call of duty during Drew's early colicky months, and to my mother and sister who took shifts watching Drew at night when I visited them; to Michelle Cudworth, Kristen Bazonski, and Stephanie Myers; to Shannon Farley and her son Quentin; and to the readers of Velveteen Rabbi and the participants in ReadWritePoem and Big Tent Poetry, who read and commented upon many of these poems in their earliest versions.

About the Author

Rachel Barenblat holds an MFA from the Bennington Writing Seminars. She is a Jewish Renewal rabbi, ordained by ALEPH: the Alliance for Jewish Renewal in January of 2011. She serves Congregation Beth Israel in North Adams, MA.

She is author of *70 Faces: Torah Poems* (Phoenicia Publishing, 2011) as well as four chapbooks of poetry: *the skies here* (Pecan Grove Press, 1995), *What Stays* (Bennington Writing Seminars Alumni Chapbook Series, 2002), *chaplainbook* (Laupe House Press, 2006) and *Through*, a self-published chapbook of miscarriage poems (2009).

Since 2003 she has blogged as The Velveteen Rabbi; in 2008, her blog was named one of the top 25 blogs on the internet by TIME. She is perhaps best known for *The Velveteen Rabbi's Haggadah for Pesach*, which has been used in homes and synagogues worldwide.

Her poems have appeared in a wide variety of magazines and anthologies, among them *Phoebe*, *The Jewish Women's Literary Annual*, *The Texas Observer*, and *Confrontation*.

She lives in the Berkshire mountains of western Massachusetts with her husband Ethan Zuckerman, their son Drew, and their creamsicle cat. You can find her online at velveteenrabbi.com.

About Phoenicia Publishing

Phoenicia Publishing is an independent press based in Montreal but involved, through a network of online connections, with writers and artists all over the world. We are interested in words and images that illuminate culture, spirit, and the human experience. A particular focus is on writing and art about travel between cultures—whether literally, through lives of refugees, immigrants, and travelers, or more metaphorically and philosophically—with the goal of enlarging our understanding of one another through universal and particular experiences of change, displacement, disconnection, assimilation, sorrow, gratitude, longing and hope.

We are committed to the innovative use of the web and digital technology in all aspects of publishing and distribution, and to making high-quality works available that might not be viable for larger publishers. We work closely with our authors, and are pleased to be able to offer them a greater share of royalties than is normally possible.

Your support of this endeavor is greatly appreciated.

Our complete catalogue is online at www.phoeniciapublishing.com

Made in the USA
Lexington, KY
28 June 2013